Bibliographic information published by the German National Library:

The German National Library lists this publication in the National Bibliography; detailed bibliographic data are available on the Internet at http://dnb.dnb.de .

Imprint:

Copyright © 2008 GRIN Verlag, Open Publishing GmbH
Print and binding: Books on Demand GmbH, Norderstedt Germany
ISBN: 9783668443112

This book at GRIN:

http://www.grin.com/en/e-book/356266/knowledge-discovery-in-data-with-selected-java-open-source-software

Carlos Rojas, Olfa Nasraoui, Nurcan Durak, Leyla Zhuhadar, et al.

Knowledge Discovery in Data with selected Java Open Source Software

GRIN Publishing

GRIN - Your knowledge has value

Since its foundation in 1998, GRIN has specialized in publishing academic texts by students, college teachers and other academics as e-book and printed book. The website www.grin.com is an ideal platform for presenting term papers, final papers, scientific essays, dissertations and specialist books.

Visit us on the internet:

http://www.grin.com/

http://www.facebook.com/grincom

http://www.twitter.com/grin_com

Contents

Knowledge Discovery in Data with selected Java Open Source Software[*]

Carlos Rojas   Olfa Nasraoui   Nurcan Durak   Leyla Zuhadar

Sofiane Sellah   Zhiyong Zhang   Basheer Hawwash

Esin Saka   Elizabeth Leon   Jonatan Gomez   Fabio Gonzalez   Maha Soliman

Abstract

We give an overview of our experience in utilizing several open source packages and composing them into sophisticated applications to solve several challenging problems as part of some of the research projects at the Knowledge Discovery & Web Mining lab at the Universe of Louisville. The projects have a common theme of knowledge discovery, however their application domains span a variety of areas. These areas range from mining Web data streams to mining Astronomy related image data, as well as Web information retrieval in social multimedia websites and e-learning platforms. As is already known, a significant proportion of the effort in any real life project involving knowledge discovery in data (KDD) is devoted to the early and final stages of KDD, i.e., the data collection and preprocessing, and the visualization of the results. Given the nature of the data in our projects, we expose our experience in handling text data and image data as part of the KDD process. In addition to the open source packages that we used, we will briefly present some of the stand-alone software that we developed in the lab, in particular a suite of software for clustering and for stream data mining.

1 Introduction

Among the most interesting features of the Web is the ease with which an individual or group can publish documents, and make them available to everyone. In the case of software this is an astonishing feat, because it means that one can access almost immediately an immense body of working programs and applications. Moreover, as it has happened with the Open Source initiative, the Web has facilitated the cooperation of collaborators scattered around the globe.

We give an overview of our experience in utilizing several open source packages as part of some of the research projects

at the Knowledge Discovery & Web Mining lab at the Universe of Louisville. We present with different degrees of detail our projects on mining solar images (Section 2), evolutionary and stream clustering techniques (Section 3), pattern discovery from transactional data streams (Section 4), an open source search engine-based recommender system (Section 5), an integrated engine for image and text search (Section 6), and an enriched search for E-learning (Section 7). In Section 8 we discuss the stages of the knowledge discovery process where we have used some of the Open Source tools. Finally, we conclude our paper in Section 9.

2 Mining Solar Images to Support Astrophysics Research

Motivation: In order to study several problems, such as the coronal heating problem, astrophysicists need many samples containing rare instances of coronal loops. Unfortunately, the identification of these images from online repositories is still done manually, which makes it very tedious and time consuming, thus slowing down the advance of science in this field.

Data: The data for this project is captured by measuring instruments onboard several orbiting satellites that are directed at the Sun. It is publicly available on `http://umbra.nascom.nasa.gov/eit/` in the case of EIT [1], and on `http://trace.lmsal.com/` in the case of TRACE[2].

Our approach: In this project, funded by NASA, and by NSF, we work on developing an image retrieval system based on Data Mining to quickly sift through massive data sets downloaded from online NASA solar image databases and to automatically discover the rare but interesting images containing a special solar event that occurs above the surface of the sun, known as coronal loops, and essential in studies of

---

[*]At the time of this work, the authors were with the Knowledge Discovery & Web Mining Lab, Dept. of Computer Science and Engineering, University of Louisville, Louisville, KY 40292,USA. Elizabeth Leon, Jonatan Gomez and Fabio Gonzalez are with the Computer Systems & Industrial Engineering Dept., National University of Colombia, Bogota, Colombia.

[1]EIT: Extreme ultraviolet Imaging Telescope on board Solar and Heliospheric Observatory (SOHO): http://umbra.nascom.nasa.gov/eit/

[2]TRACE: Transition Region and Coronal Explorer is a NASA Small Explorer (SMEX) mission to image the solar corona and transition region at high angular and temporal resolution. (http://trace.lmsal.com/)

the Coronal Heating Problem. The project aims at retrieving solar images with coronal loops from online solar image databases such as EIT [3] and TRACE[4]. We rely on image processing and classification techniques to detect images having loop shapes and to locate the coronal loops. The characteristics of coronal loops are captured via several image based features to be trained by various classifiers. The model generated from the best classifier is used in the final coronal loop retrieval application to determine which images, out of a collection of input images, contain coronal loops. The input to the system is a set of images and the output is a list of images having coronal loops and the positions of the coronal loops on the retrieved images. We have presented our results in [1]. Our solar loop mining tool is called *SOLOMON* (SOlar LOop Mining for ONline collections), and uses the following Java Open Source packages:

1. ImageJ[5]: ImageJ is a public domain Java image processing program inspired by NIH Image for the Macintosh.

2. Weka[6]: Weka is a collection of machine learning algorithms for data mining tasks available through a GNU General Public License.

Training Phase of SOLOMON Training starts with an expert-marked solar image data set. For every image, the circumference of the solar disk is divided into blocks. Blocks are labeled automatically as *Loop* if they intersect with any marked loop region, and as *No-Loop* otherwise. After block labeling, specialized image features are extracted from both types of regions, i.e. with and without a loop shape. Then using these extracted features, various classifiers are trained to distinguish *Loop* blocks from *No-Loop* blocks. The flow chart of the training phase is shown in Figure 1.

Preprocessing We start by downloading FITS images in the 171 A^o wavelength, from NASA's EIT repository, then we apply preprocessing techniques such as median filtering, Sobel edge detection, global thresholding, and skeletonization methods to remove noise and enhance contours. These steps are performed using ImageJ.

Feature Extraction After preprocessing, we divide the solar circumference into regions that we call blocks. A block is defined by its position, height, and width values. These blocks are then labeled as either containing solar loops (i.e.,

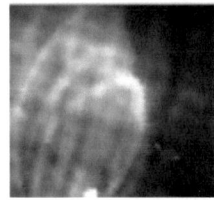 

(a) Intensity Level Block (b) Binary Level Block

Figure 2: Intensity (a) and Binary (b) Level Blocks

Loop class), or not (i.e. NO-loop class). Features are extracted from both intensity level and binary level blocks. A sample of the intensity level and binary level versions of a 'Loop' block are shown in Figure 2.

The features are extracted from each block separately. From the intensity level versions, the following statistical features are extracted: *'Mean'*, *'Standard Deviation'*, *'Smoothness'*, *'Third Moment'*, *'Uniformity'*, and *'Entropy'*. The remaining features are extracted from the binary level blocks. The *'Number of Edge Pixels'* is the total number of pixels located on all the edges in the binary blocks. From the Hough transform of the binary blocks, we acquire two features: *'Number of Hough Lines'* and *'Length of Longest Hough Line'* which is the number of points in the global maximum of the Hough Space. Since the directions of the lines in the blocks seemed to be discriminating features, we also computed Edge Histogram descriptors (*'Number of Vertical Edges'*, *'Number of Horizontal Edges'*, *'Number of 45° Edges'*, *'Number of 135° Edges'*, and *'Number of Non-Directional Edges'*). Considering the distinct spatial edge distribution inside the Loop blocks, we further divided the block into four horizontal bands, and extracted the above edge features from each band separately. Furthermore, we applied our specially designed curve tracing algorithm on all blocks to extract potential loop curves from the midst of other kinds of undesired curves, and computed *Curvature Strength-related features*.

Training Classifiers Based on a training data set containing 403 Loop blocks and 7200 No-loop blocks, we trained several classifier models using WEKA, and obtained the results listed in Table 1, which are based on 10-fold cross-validation.

Image Based Testing Phase of SOLOMON To retrieve solar images containing loop shapes from the EIT solar image repositories, a similar process to the training part is first applied on unmarked (i.e. unlabeled) test images. After preprocessing, block generation, and feature extraction, we applied the best performing classifier model, Adaboost (using C4.5 Decision Trees as a base classifier). The final decision for an image was then made based on the predicted labels of

[3]EIT: Extreme ultraviolet Imaging Telescope on board Solar and Heliospheric Observatory (SOHO): http://umbra.nascom.nasa.gov/eit/
[4]TRACE: Transition Region and Coronal Explorer is a NASA Small Explorer (SMEX) mission to image the solar corona and transition region at high angular and temporal resolution. (http://trace.lmsal.com/)
[5]ImageJ: http://rsbweb.nih.gov/ij/
[6]Weka: http://www.cs.waikato.ac.nz/ml/weka/

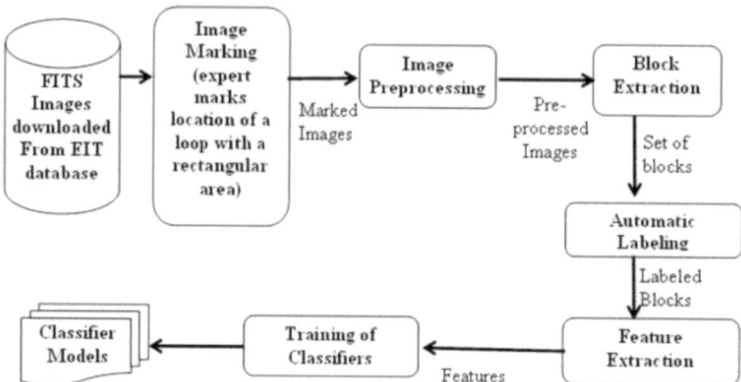

Figure 1: System Structure of SOLOMON Training Phase

Classifier	Precision	Recall
AdaBoost (C4.5)	0.63	0.662
Naive Bayes	0.363	0.768
Multi Layer Perceptron	0.621	0.694
C4.5	0.568	0.563
RIPPER	0.623	0.696
K-NN(k=5)	0.644	0.615

Table 1: Block based Cross Validation Results

Best performing image-based classifier	Precision	Recall
AdaBoost (C4.5)	0.80	0.78

Table 2: Image-based Testing Results on an independent set of online images

the blocks inside the image. If at least one block is predicted as a loop, then the image is classified into the loop class. We finally show all the predicted loop regions on the image based on the location of their Loop blocks, as shown in Figure 3. Consecutive blocks that are classified as loop blocks are merged into a bigger block that is displayed on the output image.

To evaluate the final image retrieval tool, we used images without any markings from the same years as the training data set. The testing set contained 100 images, 50 with coronal loops and 50 without any coronal loops. The final loop mining results are shown in Table 2.

System Implementation: In SOLOMON, both training and testing use the same preprocessing, block extraction, and feature extraction modules. The testing phase, however, has a different interface for the end users who cannot access the training modules. We developed an image downloading tool which connects to the EIT online database and downloads

FITS images specified by users from the database, based on their wavelength and date range criteria. We have furthermore developed an additional Coronal Loop Marking tool and patched this tool into ImageJ as a plug-in, to allow our expert-markers to mark the coronal loop regions on the solar images to be used in training. The marked regions were then saved into the FITS image file, by adding their coordinates in the FITS header, which allows them to be read and used by the block labeling module. The preprocessing phase uses mostly operators that are patched into ImageJ. After preprocessing, we divided the images into blocks and labeled them using the markings saved in the FITS format. We have also developed a Block Viewing Tool to enable viewing the blocks and their labels separately.

In the Feature Extraction phase, we extracted statistical features using several function that were already embedded in ImageJ, and implemented the rest of the features in Java. We saved the extracted feature values from each block along with the label information into an arff file which will later serve as the input to WEKA's training modules. In addition, we implemented the final Image Retrieval Tool in Java with options to load different classifier models for classification. In addition to a classifier model, the inputs to this tool are a set of images, of which the tool will output only the images having coronal loops along with the loop locations on these images.

Issues in Open Source Adoption: One limitation of ImageJ, is that it does not provide users to change parameters during the coding for most functions when we call these functions from our own Java code. This includes the default edge detection method, and the size of the median filter masks. Another limitation is the lack of sample code and online discussion forums to support developers having problems. Also, some of the function documentation was not very good.

3

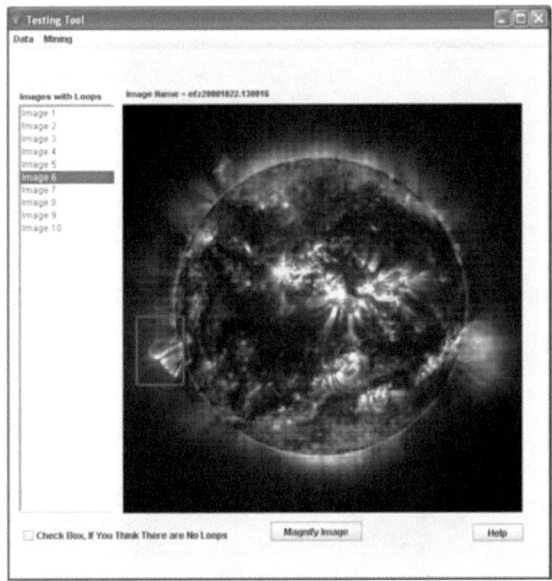

Figure 3: Snapshot of Solar Loop Mining Tool

One drawback of WEKA is its slow performance for certain classifiers such as MLP and Adaboost, particularly if the training data is very big. Adaboost may consume between 15 and 30 minutes on a typical Windows workstation (e.g, Pentium 4, with 3 Ghz and 2 GB of memory), and if we run WEKA on the same training file with different classifiers, the performance decreases further after the first classifier, and may run out of memory unexpectedly. Another limitation is that visualizing the ROC curves of several classifiers on the same output is possible with the Knowledge Flow tool of WEKA, but is not possible with the Explorer tool.

3 Evolutionary and Stream Clustering Techniques

Motivation: Clustering is an important task in knowledge discovery that aims at revealing the hidden structure of an unlabeled data set, typically by partitioning a large data set into groups of similar data called clusters, and by providing descriptions of these clusters in terms of the original features of the data set. Clustering has found successful applications in many domains, ranging from automated taxonomy generation from large text collections to discovering Web user profiles from large access log data. However, many challenges remain open in clustering. These include the difficulty to handle large data sets, noise, and the difficulty to determine the number of clusters automatically.

Data: Most of the synthetic data for this project is publicly available on our website http://webmining.spd. louisville.edu/NSF_Career/datasets.htm. Some of the benchmark real data sets used in our experiments to demonstrate performance and success are publicly available on the UCI Machine Learning Repository http:// archive.ics.uci.edu/ml/. However we have had to be very careful in sharing our real data sets used for Web Usage Mining experiments because of privacy concerns. In general, some of this data is definitely private, and the authority to share it rests with the website owners. However, we plan to sanitize some of the Web log data in such a way that no private information (such as IP addresses) remains. Instead private information will be indexed and obfuscated, leaving only the part of the data (anonymous Web requests) that has no privacy issues left, thus enabling experiments on Web usage mining to be conducted without any risks to the Website users. This data will be made available on http://webmining.spd.louisville.edu/NSF_ Career/datasets.htm.

Our approach: We developed a family of techniques in Java under the umbrella of the NSF CAREER Award: *New Clustering Algorithms Based on Robust Estimation and Genetic Niches with Applications to Web Usage Mining*. The goals of this project are listed below, and a description of the techniques follows this list.

- Mining an unknown number of clusters in the presence of a significant amount of noise

- Mining evolving user profiles to represent the users' browsing activity on a website.

- Maintaining the currency and accuracy of the Web usage profiles over time.

- Enhancing the scalability of the Web usage mining in the presence of very large Web log data sets.

- Handling the evolution of the input usage data resulting from the dynamic nature of the Web.

The Unsupervised Niche Clustering Algorithm (UNC)
The Unsupervised Niche Clustering (UNC) is an algorithm for unsupervised robust clustering based on genetic niching as an optimization strategy. It uses a Genetic Algorithm (GA) to evolve a population of candidate solutions through generations of competition and reproduction. Unlike most other clustering algorithms, UNC can handle noise in the data and can automatically determine the number of clusters. In addition, evolutionary optimization allows the use of any domain-specific optimization criterion and any similarity measure. In particular a subjective measure that exploits domain knowledge or ontologies (as was used for example for web usage mining). However, unlike purely evolutionary search-based algorithms, UNC combines evolution with local Piccard updates to estimate the scale

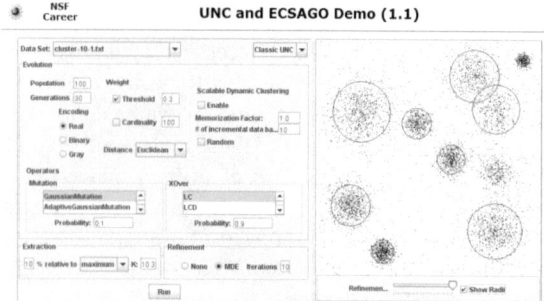

Figure 4: UNC Snapshot

of each profile, thus converging fast (about 20 generations). UNC has been successfully used, for instance, in anomaly detection [2], and in clustering spatial data sets [3]. It has been implemented from scratch first in C, then in Java. A snapshot of an online applet implementing UNC is shown in Figure 4. This applet is available on our demo website `http://webmining.spd.louisville.edu/NSF_Career/software/clustering/ECSAGO/demo/`.

The Hierarchical Unsupervised Niche Clustering Algorithm (HUNC)   HUNC is a divisive hierarchical version of **UNC**. The implementation of the HUNC algorithm exists in C (older version) and in Java (recent version). All HUNC modules are developed in-house. HUNC is described in [4], and a complete framework and a real case study is presented in [5]. HUNC has proved its effectiveness when compared to other clustering methodologies. In a recent experiment, HUNC profiles were compared to the profiles resulting from traditional pattern discovery, where the entire usage data from all time periods is used to discover usage patterns in one shot. The latter can be considered as the best output possible since all usage data is mined at once. However, HUNC has proved that it too can discover profiles that are as good (or better) than using the traditional one-shot method. Most importantly, HUNC has the critical advantage of enabling scalability in handling very large usage data that makes it impossible to mine all patterns in one shot. A snapshot of the HUNC interface is shown in Figure 5. HUNC can be described as follows

Input: Web Logs (ex: 122.33.124.128 - - [22/Jan/1998:14:19:35   -0600]   "GET   /faculty.html HTTP/1.0" 304 -)

Output: A set of profiles where each profile consist of a set of URLs with their weight. A sample profile is shown in Figure 7.

Preprocessing Module: the web logs are cleaned by removing all irrelevant requests such as image requests, requests from search agents, and unsuccessful requests. Then the page requests are grouped into units called sessions,

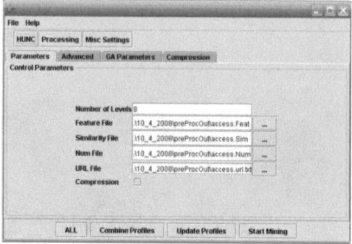

(a) Pre-Processing Screen

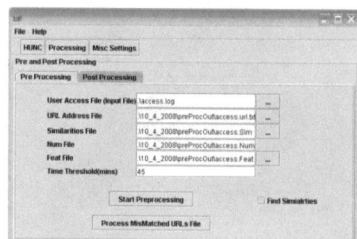

(b) Mining Screen

Figure 5: HUNC Snapshot

where each session represents all the pages visited by a particular user within a predefined period of time. Moreover, a URL index (URL Map) is created that includes all the URLs accessed in the web logs. This map is kept through future pattern discovery phases, and is always updated to reflect new URLs in the web site.

Updating Profiles: The new sessions at time t_i are compared against profiles generated at time t_{i-1}. All unique sessions (Distinct Sessions) at t_i will go through the HUNC mining module. The matching sessions at t_i are used to update the profiles from t_{i-1} which result in the Updated Profiles at t_i.

HUNC Mining: the HUNC Algorithm is used to discover new clusters at t_i from the distinct sessions at t_i .

Post Processing: The sessions in the input data set are matched to the closest cluster, and their URL frequencies are summarized by averaging over all sessions in the cluster. The set of all these URLs and their frequency of access in the same cluster constitute the cluster Profile. This generates a set of New Distinct Profiles at t_i.

Combine Profiles: Combine the updated profiles at t_i and the newly discovered profiles at t_i into one set of profiles which will serve as the Seed Profiles for the next mining cycle at t_{i+1}.

Other clustering algorithms   In addition to HUNC, we have developed the following in-house clustering algorithms.

1. ECSAGO (Evolutionary Clustering with Self Adaptive Genetic Operators) and Scalable ECSAGO (in Java): These algorithms are an extension of **UNC** to use self

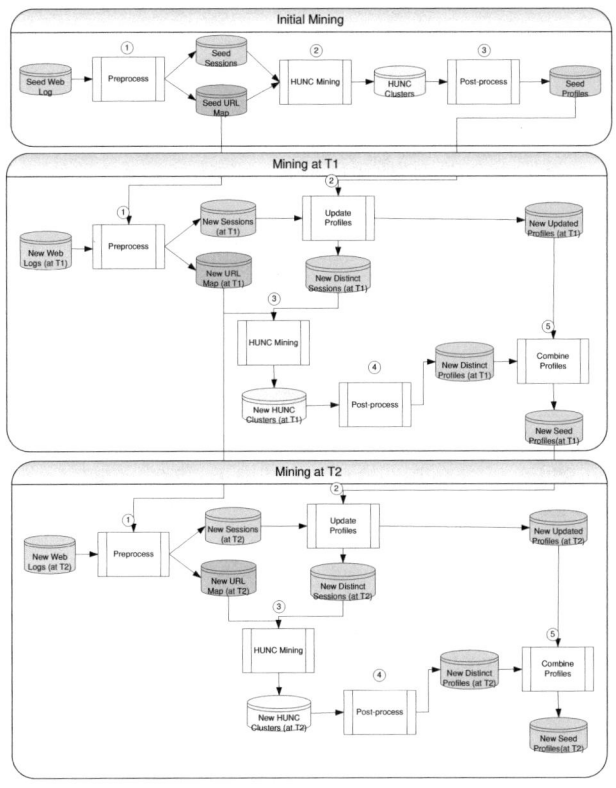

Figure 6: Evolutionary Clustering Methodology

```
Profile:  9, Num.URLS: 11, Cardinality:  58
StartDate:  30/Jan/1998:17:30:33 , End Date:
04/Feb/1998:13:37:34 , Variance:  0.0857
{0.98 - /courses.html}
{0.98 - /courses100.html}
{0.96 - /courses_index.html}
{0.82 - /}
{0.74 - /cecs_computer.class}
{0.34 - /courses300.html}
{0.20 - /courses200.html}
{0.17 - /courses_webpg.html}
{0.12 - /~joshi/courses/cecs352}
{0.10 - /courses400.html}
{0.10 - /people.html}
```

Figure 7: Sample Profile

adaptive genetic operators that dynamically determine the optimal crossover and mutation rates throughout the evolution process. ECSAGO is a single-batch version, while Scalable ECSAGO is a scalable multi-batch data streaming version. A Java applet impementing both algorithms is available on our demo website http://webmining.spd.louisville.edu/NSF_ Career/software/clustering/ECSAGO/demo/. More details can be found in [6] with successful application to anomaly detection, in particular, network intrusion detection and success on several benchmark machine learning data sets.

2. TECNO-STREAMS (Tracking Evolving Clusters in NOisy data STREAMS): a scalable clustering algorithm that can discover clusters in a single pass over a dynamic data stream. This algorithm uses an optimization method that is inspired by the natural Immune System. It was implemented in Java, and published in [7], and is implemented entirely in Java without any open source adoptions.

3. TRAC-STREAMS (TRacking Adaptive Clusters in data STREAMS): a scalable clustering algorithm that can discover clusters in a single pass over a dynamic data stream. This algorithm uses an optimization method based on alternating gradient-based hill climbing, combined with Chebyshev hypothesis testing for outlier detection, and for merging compatible clusters. It was implemented in C and Matlab, and published in [8].

Issues in Open Source Adoption: Our clustering algorithms are implemented in-house, so we had no issues with open source adoption. On the other hand, we plan to make our source code available through our website via a GNU open source license.

4 Pattern Discovery from Transactional Data Streams

In this project, we focus on analyzing evolving streams of transactional data to discover patterns. In data streams, very large amounts of data are generated during a short time. Data streams can be observed in, for example, the activity of mobile phone networks; the interaction between users, advertisement servers and web publishers; Internet traffic; dynamic text collections, such as e-mail, chats, blogs or news. A particular type of data streams are *evolving* data streams, that reflect ever-changing environments, like e-mail spamming, web usage patterns, or news reports.

Motivation: The nature of data streams adds many difficulties to pattern discovery tasks. In a stream context,

6

space and computational time become critical, nonnegotiable, and scarce resources, thus typically requiring online (incremental) processing, and very small memory (compared to the whole stream). In many cases, the underlying patterns change frequently (e.g., new web pages are added and deleted constantly, and the users themselves learn to interact better with the website) making obsolete what has been discovered from previously collected data. Thus, knowledge discovery techniques that are well suited for these challenges should be able to quickly evaluate current data against the recent past, recognize patterns already seen as well as novelties, and swiftly forget the patterns that the new data no longer supports.

Our approach: Our general approach is to maintain a dynamic memory of the stream, which is constantly updated based on the arriving records, and to maintain a model that reflects the relevant interactions between attributes. Relevant interactions are determined based on statistical tests, such as χ^2 and correlation tests, or on information measures. We applied our approach to the analysis of RSS news feeds and the analysis of newsgroup messages to automatically discover *topics*, defined as sets of keywords that consistently co-occur. We have also applied them to web logs and system audit logs.

Data: We have used mostly text collections, which have the advantages of easy acquisition, including custom collection of the data, and the interpretability of the results. We have used the 20 Newsgroups[7], taking advantage of the rarely used timestamps. Because this data is well known and acceptably accurate, it is possible to build specific scenarios (e.g. mild or strong dynamics) to evaluate our techniques and parameters. We have also collected and used New York Times RSS feeds, and system audit and web logs.

Preprocessing: Because there is no option for repeated passes over the data, preprocessing is limited to quick and simple operations. For example, in our application to text documents, pruning based on frequency is always referred to the current memory, not to global counts. Also, stemming and stop word removal are the vocabulary reduction techniques we use that incorporate some domain knowledge.

Pattern Discovery: Our published work ([9]) includes the use of a dynamic prefix tree as memory, and a graph of relevant attribute co-occurrences as model, extracted periodically using an information-based criterion. We have also used sliding windows as a memory mechanism (based on time and number of records), and an approximation of the

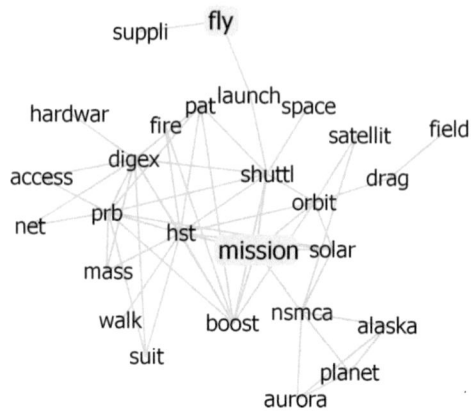

Figure 8: Example of topic visualization.

distribution of the attribute interactions as a model that is updated permanently.

Visualization: Because our models are based on interactions between attributes, they can be visualized using graphs, which helps to interpret the results. We use the Prefuse visualization toolkit (described below) for this purpose. An example of this visualization is shown in Figure 8, for a topic related to space.

Software: We have implemented our pattern discovery algorithms in Java. Besides, we use the following Java Open Source packages:

- JDOM[8]: "...robust, light-weight means of reading and writing XML data...". Apache-style open source license.

- ROME (RSS and Atom utilities)[9]: "...set of open source Java tools for parsing, generating and publishing RSS and Atom feeds...". Built on top of **JDOM**. It has an Apache 2.0 Licensing. We use it for retrieving and extracting text from the RSS feeds.

- Snowball[10]: Open Source (Java, C, and others) implementations of the Porter Stemmer for various languages, with a BSD License. We use it to perform stemming and stop word removal.

- Prefuse Visualization Toolkit[11]: "a set of software tools for creating rich interactive data visualizations. The Prefuse toolkit provides a visualization framework for the Java programming language". Also with a BSD License. Prefuse uses **Lucene**, explained in Section 6.

---

[7]20 Newsgroups dataset `http://kdd.ics.uci.edu/databases/20newsgroups/20newsgroups.html`

[8]JDOM: `www.jdom.org/`
[9]ROME: `https://rome.dev.java.net/`
[10]Snowball: `http://snowball.tartarus.org/`
[11]Prefuse `http://prefuse.org/`

Issues in Open Source Adoption: In general, the major difficulty was to find the best way to use the packages, because documentation is sketchy in many cases. Another problem is that, occasionally, the projects are not completely stable, and newer versions are not necessarily backward compatible. However, once an Open Source package was incorporated in the process, the benefit was clear; the applications are usually well written and, thanks to the community effort, better than what could be expected from a single person trying to solve a complex problem completely on their own.

5 Open Source Search Engine-based Recommender System for Multiple Websites

Motivation: Our motivation was the difficulty in implementing Web recommender systems from scratch, particularly when this had to be done very fast for experimentation purposes. Thus our goal is to easily "implement" (existing) recommendation strategies by using a search engine software when it is available, and thus to benefit research and real life applications by taking advantage of search engines' scalable and built-in indexing and query matching features, instead of implementing a strategy from scratch. Thus we developed an application that has the following benefits:

- Multi-Website Integration by Dynamic Linking enabling: (i) dynamic, personalized, and automated linking of partnering or affiliated websites, (ii) Crawling several websites and connecting them through a common proxy

- Giving Control Back to the User or Community (who can set up their own proxy) instead of the website/business

- Taking advantage of the Open Source edge

- Tapping into the established Information Retrieval / Web search legacy.

Our approach: We developed a systematic framework for a fast and easy implementation and deployment of a recommendation system that works on one or several affiliated or subject-specific websites, and based on any available combination of open source tools that includes: **(i)** crawling, **(ii)** indexing, and **(iii)** searching capabilities. A detailed description with some experiments showing success can be found in [10, 11]. The system can provide on-the-fly recommendation for web surfers based on their clickstream data which are transformed into a dynamic user session profile. The recommendations consist of links to pages contained within a given collection of websites that have been previously indexed. The system uses a search engine behind the scene to search for pages that are similar to the user's profile by formulating an implicit query automatically from the user's profile. An inverted index must have been previously formed by crawling, parsing and indexing several participating websites, thus accelerating the recommendation process.

Software: Our implementation is based mostly on open source modules, and is explained in detail on `http://webmining.spd.louisville.edu/open-source-recommender/index.html`. The architecture is shown in Figure 9. We use the following open source components:

- Squid Proxy Cache: We used Version Squid 2.5.STABLE12.

- Nutch Search Engine: Currently we are using version nutch-0.6.

In addition, we implemented our own Recommender System Module in C, which can be downloaded from `http://webmining.spd.louisville.edu/open-source-recommender/codes/recommender.tar.gz`.

Issues in Open Source Adoption: We have had to make several changes to the open source components to make them useful for our purpose. These changes include a modified "client_side.c" code for Squid, and the changed code can be downloaded from our website at `http://webmining.spd.louisville.edu/open-source-recommender/codes/client_side.c`. In order for nutch to support similar page query and termvector query, we modified nutch's source code. Our new source code can be downloaded from our website at `http://webmining.spd.louisville.edu/open-source-recommender/nutch/nutch-0.6_rec.tar.gz`. Also, a list of the changes that we made is available on `http://webmining.spd.louisville.edu/open-source-recommender/nutch/changes.html`.

6 Show And Tell: A Seamlessly Integrated Image and Text Search Engine.

Show And Tell, published in [12], is a Web based image search tool that combines keyword and image content feature querying and search. We used the following Java Open Source packages:

1. Lucene[12]: "Apache Lucene is a high-performance, full-featured text search engine library written entirely in Java. It is a technology suitable for nearly any application that requires full-text search, especially cross-platform".

---

[12]Lucene: `http://lucene.apache.org/`

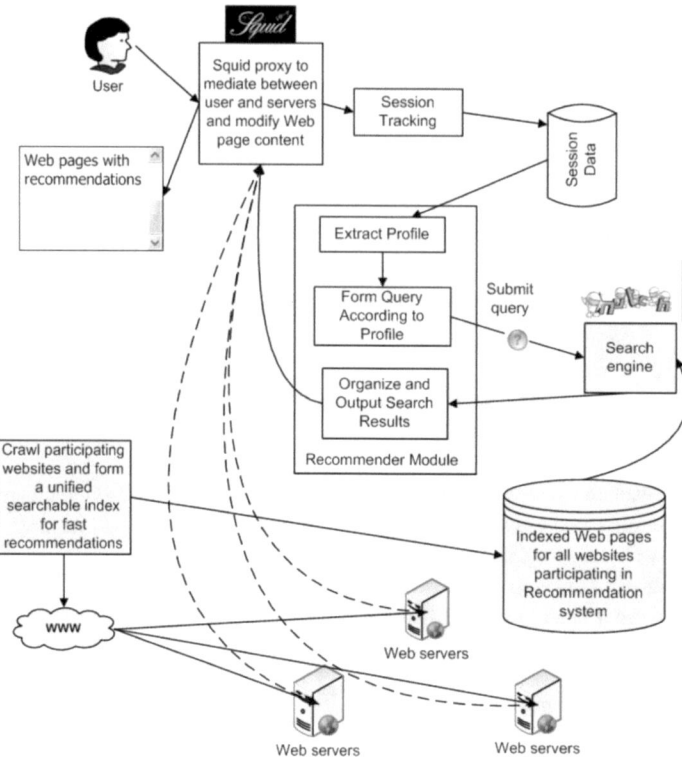

Figure 9: System Architecture of the open source search-engine-based recommender system.

2. Nutch[13]: Apache "Nutch is an open source web-search software. It builds on **Lucene** Java, adding web-specifics, such as a crawler, a link-graph database, parsers for HTML, and other document formats, etc."

Data: Most of the data for this project is publicly available by crawling various social multimedia websites such as Flickr http://www.flickr.com/.

7 Personalized Cluster-based Semantically Enriched Web Search for E-learning:

In this project, we developed an approach for personalized search in an e-learning platform, that takes advantage of semantic Web standards (RDF[14] and OWL[15]) to represent the content and the user profiles, and then using the learner's context to improve the precision and recall in e-learning search, particularly by re-ranking the search results based on the learner's past activities (profile). Our model consists of the following algorithms: (1) bottom-up pruning algorithm to building the learner's semantic profile, (2)

learner-to-best cluster mapping algorithm, and (3) re-ranking a learner's search results. **Nutch** is embedded in our "Hyper-ManyMedia" [16] platform so that online students could fetch many different media format resources: text, MS Power-Point, audio, video, podcast, and vodcast of online resources (lectures). Additionally, we use:

1. Protégé[17]: a Java-based ontology editor and knowledge-base framework. "The Protégé platform supports two main ways of modeling ontologies, via the Protégé-Frames and Protégé-OWL editors. Protégé ontologies can be exported into a variety of formats including RDF, OWL, and XML Schema". Mozilla Public License (MPL).

2. Cluto[18]: a clustering package. We use it to cluster the complete e-Learning domain textual contents. The resulting clusters can later be used to determine each learner's semantic profile. The cluster centroids (keywords) are used both to provide recommendation terms for a specific learner during search, and to add the key-

---

[13]Nutch: http://lucene.apache.org/nutch/
[14]Resource Description Framework (RDF) http://www.w3.org/RDF/
[15]OWL Web Ontology Language http://www.w3.org/TR/owl-features/

[16]WKU HyperManyMedia Distance Learning Platform: http://blog.wku.edu/podcasts
[17]Protégé: http://protege.stanford.edu/
[18]Cluto: http://glaros.dtc.umn.edu/gkhome/cluto/cluto/overview

9

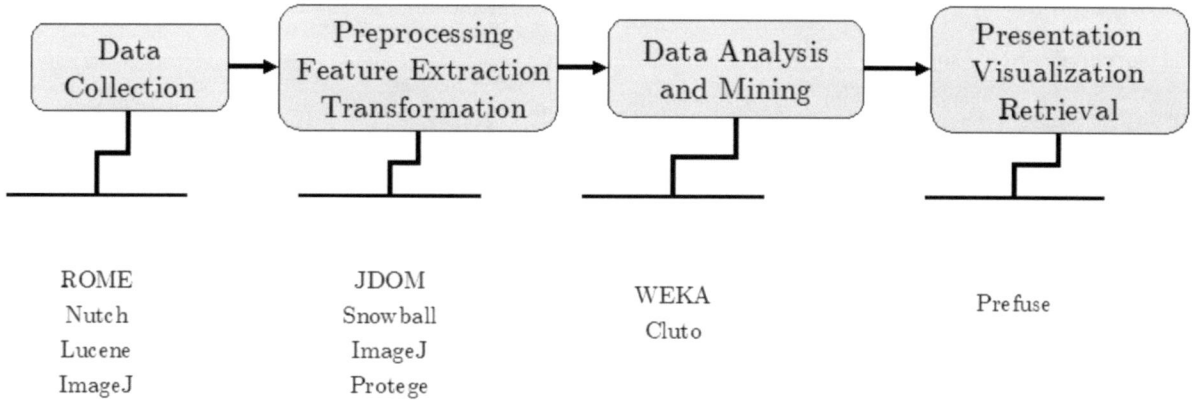

Figure 10: Open Source packages in the KDD process in our projects.

words to the domain ontology as subclass relations. This is publicly available software, but not open source, and free to use in a research environment.

Data: Most of the data for this project is publicly available on WKU's hyper-many media e-learning platform `http://161.6.105.103:8084/nutch-0.9/manymediaplatform.html`.

8 Open Source packages in the KDD process.

As is already known, a significant proportion of the effort in any real life project involving knowledge discovery in data (KDD) is devoted to the early and final stages of KDD, i.e., the data collection and preprocessing, and the visualization of the results. We use them mostly in tasks where well known methods exist, and consequently, there are good Open Source tools available. The following diagram summarizes the packages that we have used, and where they fit in the KDD process. This diagram does not include our own software that was developed in-house, such as the evolutionary clustering and stream clustering algorithms. However this software will be made available through a suitable open source license in the near future, on our wesbite `http://webmining.spd.louisville.edu/NSF_Career/software/software_clustering.htm`. In general, our in-house software touches all the phases of the KDD process.

9 Summary and conclusions.

We have described a variety of projects in which the Knowledge Discovery & Web Mining lab at the University of Louisville has been involved, and we have described the Open Source tools that we have adopted to our purposes. Below, we list certain issues and lessons that we have gathered from these endeavors, besides what was mentioned in the individual projects above.

- At times several Open Source projects attempt to solve the same problem. It is important to be careful in picking the right tool not only in the sense of solving the problem at hand, but also the one that is probably going to be healthy for the duration of the project.

- Open Source tools are completely the opposite of black boxes. They invite the developer to explore them, to change them, and to be an active user (or contributor), rather than just a consumer.

- They are Open Source tools, and in many cases free, but they are *not work-free*, in the sense that one should expect a certain degree of time investment in understanding the tool; and if more complex tasks are required, one must be capable of digging into the code and willing to do it.

- There are a variety of licensing schemes. For research purposes, there are generally no restrictions. However, for commercial purposes, one should read the details, but there are plenty of opportunities if one so wishes. For example, Apache 2.0 licensing allows commercial use, and does not require the additions to be Open Source.

- It is important to try to contribute. Open Source tools are possible because of the good will and skill of competent people who are willing to give their work virtually for free. If one is using those tools, one is probably skilled enough to give some feedback, and thus be a useful contributor to the Open Source community.

10

Acknowledgment

This work was partially supported by the National Aeronautics and Space Administration under Grant No. AISR-03-0077-0139 issued through the Office of Space Sciences, by the National Science Foundation CAREER Award IIS-0133948 to O. Nasraoui, by NSF grant IIS-0431128, and by a Fellowship from the Logistics and Distribution Institute, University of Louisville, to C. Rojas.

References

[1] N. Durak and O. Nasraoui, "Feature Exploration for Mining Coronal Loops from Solar Images," in *IEEE International Conf. on Tools with Artificial Intelligence (ICTAI)'08*, 2008, to appear.

[2] E. Leon, O. Nasraoui, and J. Gómez, "Network intrusion detection using genetic clustering," in *Genetic and Evolutionary Computation Conference (GECCO 2004)*.

[3] O. Nasraoui and R. Krishnapuram, "A novel approach to unsupervised robust clustering using genetic niching," *Fuzzy Systems, 2000. FUZZ IEEE 2000. The Ninth IEEE International Conference on*, vol. 1, pp. 170–175 vol.1, May 2000.

[4] O. Nasraoui and R. Krishnapuram, "One step evolutionary mining of context sensitive associations and web navigation patterns," in *SIAM Conf. on Data Mining (SDM 2002)*.

[5] O. Nasraoui, M. Soliman, E. Saka, A. Badia, and R. Germain, "A web usage mining framework for mining evolving user profiles in dynamic web sites," *IEEE Trans. Knowledge Data Engineering (TKDE)*, vol. 20, no. 2, pp. 202–215, 2008.

[6] E. Leon, O. Nasraoui, and J. Gomez, "ECSAGO: Evolutionary Clustering with Self Adaptive Genetic Operators," in *IEEE Conf. Evolutionary Computation (CEC)*, 2006, pp. 1768–1775.

[7] O. Nasraoui, C. Cardona, C. Rojas, and F. A. González, "TECNO-STREAMS: Tracking Evolving Clusters in Noisy Data Streams with a Scalable Immune System Learning Model," in *IEEE International Conf. on Data Mining (ICDM'03)*.

[8] O. Nasraoui and C. Rojas, "Robust clustering for tracking noisy evolving data streams." in *SIAM Conf. on Data Mining (SDM 2006)*.

[9] C. Rojas and O. Nasraoui, "Summarizing Evolving Data Streams using Dynamic Prefix Trees," in *WI' 07*, 2007.

[10] O. Nasraoui, Z. Zhang, and E. Saka, "Web Recommender System Implementations in Multiple Flavors: Fast and (Care) Free for All," in *SIGIR Open Source Information Retrieval workshop*, 2006, pp. 46–53.

[11] Z. Zhang and O. Nasraoui, "Efficient Web Recommendations Based on Markov Clickstream Models and Implicit Search," in *IEEE/WIC/ACM International Conference on Web Intelligence (WI)*, 2007.

[12] Z. Zhang, C. Rojas, O. Nasraoui, and H. Frigui, "SHOW AND TELL: A Seamlessly Integrated Tool For Searching with Image Content And Text," in *ACM-SIGIR Open Source Information Retrieval workshop*, 2006.